D0811578

Alligators

A Buddy Book
by
Julie Murray

VISIT US AT
www.abdopub.com

Published by Buddy Books, an imprint of ABDO Publishing Company, 4940 Viking Drive, Suite 622, Edina, Minnesota 55435. Copyright © 2002 by Abdo Consulting Group, Inc. International copyrights reserved in all countries. No part of this book may be reproduced in any form without written permission from the publisher.

Printed in the United States.

Edited by: Christy DeVillier
Contributing Editors: Matt Ray, Michael P. Goecke
Graphic Design: Maria Hosley
Image Research: Deborah Coldiron
Photographs: Gary Braasch, Getty Images, Fotosearch

Library of Congress Cataloging-in-Publication Data

Murray, Julie, 1969-
    Alligators/Julie Murray.
        p. cm. — (Animal kingdom)
    Summary: Describes the physical characteristics, behavior and habitat of alligators.
    ISBN 1-57765-716-0
        1. Alligators—Juvenile literature. [1. Alligator.] I. Title. II. Animal kingdom (Edina, Minn.)

QL666.C925 M87 2002
597.98'4—dc21

                                                    2001053819

Contents

Alligators 4

Reptiles 6

What They Look Like 8

Where They Live 13

Hunting And Eating 14

Predators 16

Baby Alligators 18

Alligators In America 20

Important Words 22

Web Sites 23

Index .24

Alligators

Alligators have been around for millions of years. They are among the oldest predators on earth. There are two kinds of alligators: the American alligator and the Chinese alligator.

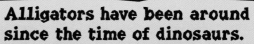

Alligators have been around since the time of dinosaurs.

Reptiles

Alligators, crocodiles, snakes, and turtles are all reptiles. Reptiles have scales and backbones. A reptile's body temperature changes with the air and water around it. When reptiles are cold, they need the sun to warm up. When reptiles are hot, they need shade or water to cool down. This is why we call reptiles cold-blooded animals.

An American alligator
warms itself in the sun.

What They Look Like

American alligators can grow very big. They can be 12 to 14 feet (3 to 4 m) long. The Chinese alligator is smaller than the American alligator. It only grows to about six feet (two m) in length. The largest alligator known was 19 feet (6 m) long!

Chinese alligators are about half the size of American alligators.

American alligator

Chinese alligator

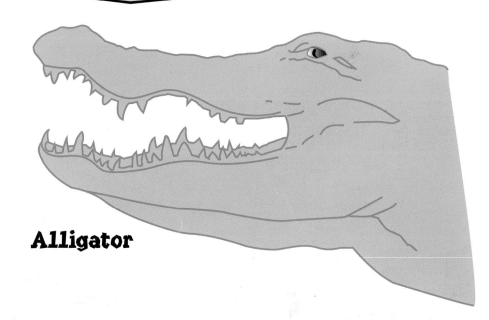

Alligator

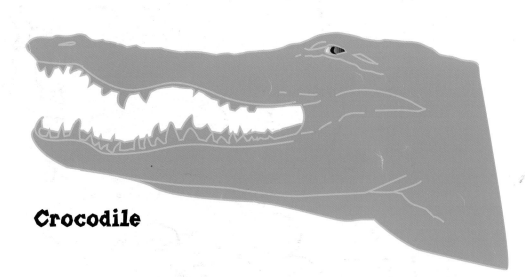

Crocodile

An alligator's long mouth is wider than a crocodile's. Alligators have webbed feet and long, powerful tails for swimming. Hard scales cover the alligator's body.

Alligators have scales all over.

Do Alligators Have Ears?

Yes, alligators do have ears. They are small slits underneath flaps of skin. They are behind the alligator's eyes. An alligator's eyes, ears, and nose are on the top of its head. So these reptiles can see, hear, and smell while floating in water.

ears

Where They Live

Alligators live in the calm waters of rivers, lakes, canals, marshes, swamps, and bayous. These reptiles go on land to nest. They lie in the sun, too.

The Chinese alligator lives in the Yangtze River Valley in China. American alligators live in the southeastern United States. Florida and Louisiana have a lot of American alligators.

Hunting
And Eating

Alligators are meat-eaters, or carnivores. Alligators eat frogs, turtles, fish, birds, muskrats, and other animals. They swallow everything without chewing.

Alligators often ambush their prey. This means they take animals by surprise. Alligators hide quietly waiting for prey. When an animal comes close, they grab it quickly. Alligators have powerful mouths for catching prey.

Alligators often lie still in water to ambush prey.

Predators

Predators of adult alligators are other alligators and people. Alligators can run very fast to escape predators. They can also fight off predators by biting. These reptiles fight with their tails, too. An alligator's strong, heavy tail can knock down a large animal.

This alligator might look like a log from far away.

Hiding is another way to guard against predators. It is not always easy to see alligators lying still in water.

Baby Alligators

Alligators lay their eggs in nests. The mother builds a nest of mud and plants. She commonly lays about 45 eggs at one time. The mother alligator covers her eggs with mud and plants. She will stay near the nest to guard her eggs. The eggs begin hatching after about nine weeks. Then, the mother helps her babies out of the nest.

A baby alligator.

A newborn alligator is about eight inches (20 cm) long. It weighs only two ounces (57 g). Baby alligators have black bodies with yellow stripes.

Alligators In America

At one time, there were millions of alligators in the United States. Over the years, people destroyed the alligator's habitat. People hunted alligators for their skins, too. So, alligators began to die out.

People made shoes, handbags, and belts from alligator skin.

Today, there are laws that keep alligators safe. Thanks to these laws, American alligators are not endangered anymore.

Important Words

ambush hiding in order to surprise something or someone.

endangered in danger of dying out.

habitat where an animal lives in the wild.

predator an animal that hunts and eats other animals.

prey an animal that is food for another animal.

reptile a cold-blooded animal with lungs, scales, and a backbone.

scales hard plates.

temperature how hot or cold something is.

Web Sites

The American Alligator

www.ifas.ufl.edu/AgriGator/gators/
You can learn more about American alligators at this web site.

Crocodiles

www.pbs.org/wgbh/nova/crocs/
Discover why crocodiles outlived dinosaurs and how smart these reptiles may be.

The Gator Hole

http://home.cfl.rr.com/gatorhole/
What is a gator hole? Find out at this fact-filled web site.

Index

ambush **15**

American alligator **4, 7, 8, 9, 13, 21**

carnivore **14**

Chinese alligator **4, 8, 9, 13**

crocodiles **6, 10, 11**

eggs **18**

endangered **21**

Florida **13**

habitat **20**

Louisiana **13**

nest **13, 18**

predator **4, 16, 17**

prey **15**

reptile **6, 12, 13, 16**

scales **6, 11**

snakes **6**

turtles **6, 14**

Yangtze River Valley, China **13**